P9-DIB-410

T 17277   What is a community? : from A to Z

307

FI

AlphaBasics

What is a
Community?
from A to Z

Bobbie Kalman

Crabtree Publishing Company

AlphaBasiCs

Created by Bobbie Kalman

For my friend Peg Buckley, a community-type gal

Author and Editor-in-Chief
Bobbie Kalman

Managing editor
Lynda Hale

Editors
Kate Calder
Heather Levigne

Computer design
Lynda Hale
Trevor Morgan (borders & letters)

Photo research
Kate Calder

Production coordinator
Hannelore Sotzek

Separations and film
Dot 'n Line Image Inc.

Printer
Worzalla Publishing Company

Special thanks to
Colonial Williamsburg Foundation; Littleton Historical Museum; Ridley College; Danny Bang; Whitney Peterson; Samantha Crabtree; Nicola Hill; Osia and Holly Wilson; Karl Baker, Michael Malaney, and Suki the dog; Peter Koitsas, Janet Eastwood

Photographs
Jim Bryant: pages 16 (top left and bottom right), 22 (top left); Marc Crabtree: pages 6 (top left), 10 (bottom left), 13 (bottom left), 14 (top left and bottom), 15 (top middle and top right), 27 (bottom right); Peter Crabtree: pages 13 (top left), 15 (bottom left); courtesy of Littleton Historical Museum: page 13 (right); Bobbie Kalman: pages 6 (bottom right), 9 (bottom left), 10 (top right), 14 (top right), 16 (top right), 20 (background); other images by Digital Stock and Eyewire.

Illustrations
Barbara Bedell: page 14
Halina Below: page 18 (bottom)
© Crabtree Publishing Company: title page, pages 4, 7, 11, 12, 18 (top), 21, 23, 29

Crabtree Publishing Company

PMB 16A
350 Fifth Avenue,
Suite 3308
New York, NY
10118

360 York Road
RR 4
Niagara-on-the-Lake
Ontario, Canada
L0S 1J0

73 Lime Walk
Headington,
Oxford
OX3 7AD
United Kingdom

Copyright © **2000 CRABTREE PUBLISHING COMPANY**.
All rights reserved. No part of this publication may be reproduced, stored in a retrieval system or be transmitted in any form or by any means, electronic, mechanical, photocopying, recording, or otherwise, without the prior written permission of Crabtree Publishing Company.

Cataloging in Publication Data

Kalman, Bobbie
What is a community?: from A to Z

(AlphaBasiCs)
Includes index.

ISBN 0-86505-384-7 (library bound) ISBN 0-86505-414-2 (pbk.)
This book is an alphabetical introduction to the basic concepts of community, such as "Buildings," "Family," "Rules," and "Working Together."

1. Community—Juvenile literature. 2. English language—Alphabet —Juvenile literature. [1. Community. 2. Alphabet.]
I. Title. II. Series: Kalman, Bobbie. AlphaBasiCs.

HM756.K35 2000   j307   LC 99-038617
                                       CIP

Contents

is for **all about communities**. A community is a group of people living in the same area and sharing goods, services, and buildings. Communities are also the places where people live. They are located in hot, dry, wet, and cold **climates**. Some communities are small villages. Others are huge cities. Communities located on the outskirts of cities are called **suburbs**. Large communities are made up of smaller ones called **neighborhoods**. This city neighborhood is a busy place!

is for **buildings**. People in a community live and work in buildings. Your home may be a house or an apartment. There are many apartment homes in an apartment building. Schools, libraries, shops, churches, temples, and hospitals are other kinds of buildings in a community. Buildings can have different shapes and sizes. Churches often have steeples, and office buildings can be more than 30 stories high! Very tall buildings are called **skyscrapers**.

(above) The downtown areas of many cities have tall office buildings. Some apartment buildings provide homes for hundreds of people.

(top right) Communities have places of worship such as churches and temples. This old church has beautifully-colored stained-glass windows and a tall steeple.

(right) Houses come in many shapes and sizes. This family home has a swimming pool in its back yard. Is your home a house or an apartment?

 is for **culture**. Culture includes history, art, music, food, and recreation. Art galleries, theaters, and museums are examples of places in a community in which you can learn about culture. Some communities have neighborhoods where many people of one **cultural heritage** live and work. Places in which people of different backgrounds live together are called **multicultural communities**.

(top left) Aboriginal peoples were the first to live in North and South America. (top right) This Japanese artist sells his masks all over the world. (left) There are Chinatowns in many big cities. (below) These girls celebrate their Caribbean culture in a lively parade.

is for **development**. Development is the growth that takes place in a community. As communities develop, they are constantly changing. Over time, the **population**, or the number of people, in a community grows. New buildings are constructed, and old buildings are **destructed**, or torn down. Write down all the ways your community has changed in the past year. Make a list of new homes, shops, or roads in your neighborhood.

is for **environment**. Every community is situated in a natural environment. The natural environment includes land, water, living things, and climate. The natural environment is often destroyed to make room for communities. Forests are cut down, and swamps and other **wetlands** are filled in with soil so houses can be built. Dirty water from factories and homes pollutes rivers and lakes and makes living things sick.

(above) Make a list of all the natural places in your community, such as parks.

(top left) Water birds, frogs, snakes, and many mammals lose their homes when wilderness areas are destroyed.

(bottom left) The natural environment is also harmed by pollution. Fumes from cars and factories make the air unsafe to breathe.

People in a community produce garbage such as plastics, glass, paper waste, and leftover food. Metal and chemical wastes are produced in **industries**. Garbage pollutes the environment. Town workers remove garbage from streets and **incinerate** it, bury it in **landfill sites**, or **recycle** it. Recycling means using something in a new way. Plastic soda bottles, for example, are melted and then used to make sturdy park benches.

Recycling reduces the amount of garbage we have to bury or burn. Protecting the natural environment is a concern for every community. How do you help the environment?

is for **family**. Families are an important part of every community. There are many kinds of families—families with two parents, single-parent families, **foster** families, and **extended** families. Each family is like a small community. Family members love, support, protect, and respect one another. They follow rules and cooperate to make one another happy. Families often share a home, food, furniture, and money.

Many families have two parents, some have one, and others have grandparents as well as parents. Some families are part of different communities such as church or cultural communities.

F is also for **food**. Without food, people in a community could not stay alive. Some small communities grow their own food, but the people in most communities buy their food in stores or supermarkets. Some of the food in supermarkets comes from faraway countries. People in a community depend on people in other communities to grow and harvest the food they buy and eat.

(top left) Milk and other dairy products come from dairy farms. (above) Rice is grown in countries such as Japan and China. (below left and right) Apples and other fruits grow in orchards and are shipped to stores.

is for **government services**. Government services provide communities with the buildings and help they need. Schools, hospitals, libraries, buses, garbage collection, and road repair are all government services. Law enforcement and firefighting are other important services. The money people pay in taxes helps operate the government services in a community.

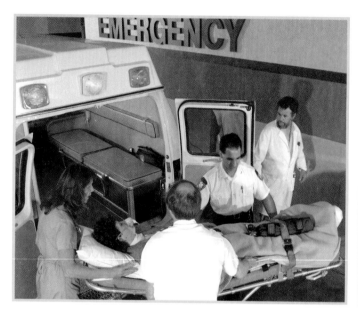

*Governments are in charge of many things. The **federal** government runs a country and makes the laws that people must follow. The **municipal** government enforces the laws in a town or city. Police officers arrest people who have committed crimes, as shown in the above right picture.*

is for **history**. History is a record of events that happened in the past. All communities have a history. By learning about the history of your country and community, you can understand more about your way of life today. **Historic communities** show us what life was like in the past. People dressed in costumes re-enact life in those early days.

The buildings in historic communities have no running water or electricity. Instead of driving in cars, people ride in wagons drawn by horses or oxen, just as they did in the past. Costumed guides show how people dressed, cooked, washed, and slept in the days of the settlers. Have you ever visited a historic community?

 is for **information**. Sending and receiving information is called **communication**. People in a community send information by speaking, writing, playing music, using signs, or drawing pictures. They receive information by watching, listening, and reading. People all over the world can communicate with one another quickly and easily on the telephone or by computer.

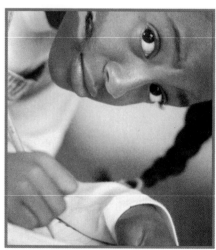

Name two ways people can send letters without going to the post office.

How do people who live on boats communicate with others?

How does this girl show her aunt she loves her?

How did people in the past who could not write advertise to those who could not read?

How can someone communicate feelings?

How are these dancers giving information about their culture to their audience?

J is for **jobs**. Jobs give people an **income**. Income is the money they earn and use to buy the things they need. Your community has many people such as doctors, teachers, and sanitary workers who do jobs that help you. Writing books, driving a truck, and serving food in a restaurant are other examples of jobs. People who own businesses provide themselves and others with jobs.

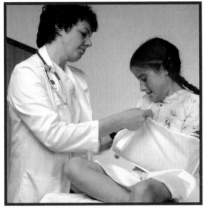

Who does these jobs?
Who brings your mail?
Who collects your garbage?
Who looks after your sick pet?
Who drives your school bus?
Who puts out fires?
Who lends you books?
Who teaches you?
Who helps you when you
are sick?

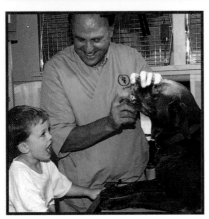

is for **kinds of communities**. Each community is different from other communities in location, climate, population, and culture. Some communities are located on islands or high up on mountains; others are in deserts or rain forests. Some have a large population, and others are made up of only a few people. Communities also differ in the ways people make their living. Farming, fishing, and tourism are some sources of income.

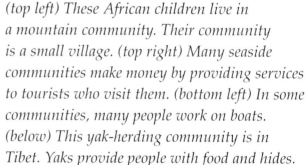

(top left) These African children live in a mountain community. Their community is a small village. (top right) Many seaside communities make money by providing services to tourists who visit them. (bottom left) In some communities, many people work on boats. (below) This yak-herding community is in Tibet. Yaks provide people with food and hides.

16

is for **learning**. People in a community are always learning new things. **Education** is the process of learning, and a school is an educational community. In school, children learn language arts, math, geography, history, and science. They are also taught how to play musical instruments and use computers. The skills children learn will help them develop a career as adults.

(above) Learning to read and write is important. Children also learn other useful subjects in school such as math, science, art, and music.

(above) This young music student loves to play the violin. Her violin teacher allows her to take it home so she can practice her music lessons every day.

(right) Industrial arts class is fun! Children learn how to make useful objects such as bird feeders.

is for **map**. A map is a diagram of a community. It helps people locate streets, parks, buildings, and bodies of water. Maps show locations of places and the distances between them. Picture maps show symbols of **landmarks**. Landmarks are important buildings, rivers, or bridges. **Legends** explain the symbols. Look at the legend shown below and find the symbols on the map next to it.

(left) This family is looking at a picture map of a park. Which symbols are used for the castle, roads, stream, trees, and parking lot?

(below) Draw a map of your school and the neighborhood around it. Use symbols to represent trees, houses, and other community buildings.

Legend:

 house

 stop sign

 park

 bridge

 gas station

 apartments

 church

 pool

 school

 playground

 river

 street lights

 bus stop

 mall

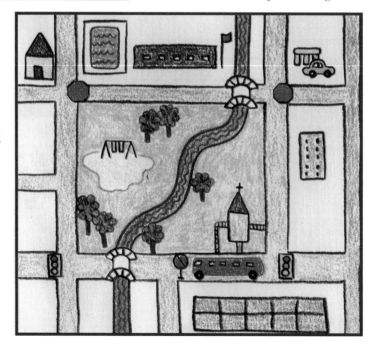

is for **newspaper**. A newspaper informs people of **current events**, or news, in their community and in communities around the world. Listening to the radio, watching television, and searching the Internet are other ways to get the news. Many communities are **interconnected**, or joined to one another, because people know what other people in faraway places are doing.

Newspapers have current events, advertisements, comics, weather news, and announcements. People watch the news on television to see important events such as space-shuttle launchings, fires and other disasters, and news about famous people.

is for **one planet**. The millions of communities around the world belong to one planet—Earth. Earth has an **atmosphere**, which is a blanket of air that surrounds the planet. All living things need air to survive. Air contains **oxygen**, which is a gas that living things breathe. It also contains a gas called **carbon dioxide** that plants use to make food. Without air, there would be no living things, nor would there be weather. Rain or snow would not fall, and wind would not blow.

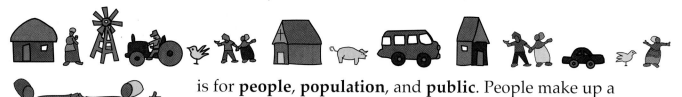

is for **people**, **population**, and **public**. People make up a community. The population is the total number of people who live there. The word public can mean the people in a community or it can describe anything that is available for use by the people who live there. Schools, swimming pools, and parks are public places. Public places are run by the government and paid by taxes. Which public places in your community do you visit often?

21

is for **quality of life**, or a standard of living. To have a good standard of living, people need food, clean water and air, clothing, shelter, and opportunities for learning and working. A good quality of life also includes getting medical care as well as help in times of emergencies such as fires. Some communities have a higher standard of living than others. Many communities do not have good housing or clean water.

Shelter, food, clothing, and community services contribute to the quality of life in a community. Quality of life varies from one community to another.

People in a community need other people for a good quality of life. They need to care for one another and have fun together. Many communities have special events such as dances, picnics, and parades that allow people to enjoy the company of others. Families and friends also have celebrations such as weddings, family reunions, and birthday parties. How did you spend your last birthday? Did you have a party?

is for **rules**. Rules help keep order in a community. You have rules in your home such as no snacks before dinner. Your school also has rules such as keeping quiet while the teacher is talking. **Laws** are rules that protect people in a community from crime. Laws also ensure that people are treated fairly. Police officers, government officials, and judges make sure that people follow the laws of a community.

These police officers patrol neighborhoods and talk to children about rules. Umpires make sure players follow the rules in baseball. Name five rules you have at school.

is for **safety**. Community workers such as firefighters, doctors, and ambulance drivers work hard to keep us safe. They protect us and help us in emergencies. We also keep ourselves safe from danger. We look both ways before crossing the road and keep away from fast-flowing rivers and strange animals. What safety tips have you learned from a firefighter or police officer in your community?

Which rules keep you safe at your community swimming pool? What do you think this police officer is saying to this boy? How can helicopters help in an emergency?

25

 is for **travel** and **transportation**. Travel is going from place to place, and transportation is the way in which people get there. People travel across land, water, or through the air. Your means of transportation can be your feet, a bicycle, car, airplane, boat, snowmobile, or hot-air balloon. Someday you might even fly aboard a space shuttle! Public transportation in a community includes buses, street cars, and trains.

*City communities often have **subways**, or underground trains. Which are the main ways of getting around your community? In how many ways do you travel during a week? Have you ever traveled to a faraway place by car, train, bus, or plane?*

is for **utilities**. Utilities are community services such as water, electricity, oil, and gas. People in a community need electricity to light their homes and operate their appliances and machines. Without electricity, we could not use our computer, listen to music, or watch television. We would have to wash our clothes by hand and read by candlelight. We use oil or gas to heat our home. Gas is also used in stoves, fireplaces, and clothes dryers.

If we did not have indoor plumbing, we would have to carry water from a well. Without gas or oil, we might have to heat our homes using wood or coal. Without electricity, people would have to make things by hand as they did in the days of the pioneers.

for **volunteers**. Volunteers are community helpers who work without being paid. Library and classroom helpers, lunchtime supervisors, and crossing guards are often volunteers. Other volunteers work in places such as hospitals and food banks. Doing volunteer work is a great experience! You can help in your school or walk dogs at an animal shelter. Being a volunteer helper in your home will make your family happy!

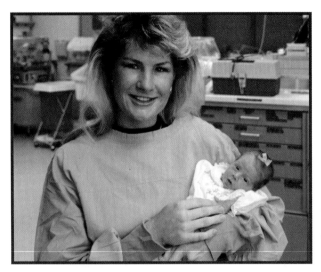

*(top left) This woman is a hospital volunteer who works with **premature** babies, or babies born too early. (bottom left) You can volunteer right at home! (right) You can volunteer to walk your dog or a neighbor's. Volunteer work will teach you how to give without expecting anything in return. Your reward will be a wonderful feeling in your heart!*

is for **working together**. The people in a community work together to make their community a better place. They depend on one another. They share buildings, goods, and services. People within a community also depend on one another for support and help. The people in this picture are cooperating to build a community swimming pool. Some are digging, and others are unloading wood and cement.

are for becoming an **expert** on **your** community. X is the second letter in expert. Y is for your community. Learn the names of the shopkeepers, fire chief, and government officials in your neighborhood. Visit the local museum to learn more about your community's history. Find out what is the main industry in your city or town. Being an expert will make you feel grateful for all the things your community provides for you.

You are an important member of your community and can enjoy all the things your community has to offer. You can join clubs that participate in community events such as picnics, bake sales, and parades. At your school, you can be an actor in a play. You can play team sports such as baseball and soccer and compete against teams from other communities. How are you involved in your community?

is for **zoos**. Zoo is short for **zoological garden**. Zoological means anything to do with animals. Many communities have zoos where animals live in areas that resemble their natural environment. Zoos help animals that are **endangered**, or in danger of dying out. They also teach people about endangered animals that live in the wild such as tigers and rhinoceroses and the problems they face.

Many zoos rescue animals that have been injured and **rehabilitate** *them so they can live in the wild again. Zoos also have breeding programs to help increase the populations of endangered animals.*

31

Words to know

aboriginal Describing people who were the first to live in an area

climate The normal long-term weather conditions in a certain area

cultural heritage A way of life that is passed from generation to generation

current events Events that are presently in the news or of interest

extended family A family including grandparents, parents, and children

foster family A family that provides care for children to whom they are not related and have not adopted

incinerate To burn until only ashes remain

industry A type of business that makes or sells goods or provides services

landfill site An area of land in which waste is buried for disposal

landmark A feature of a landscape

neighborhood A small community within a large community

recycle To turn garbage into usable items

rehabilitate To make healthy

tourism A business that provides services for visitors to a foreign country

wetland An area with waterlogged soil

Index

1 2 3 4 5 6 7 8 9 0   Printed in the U.S.A.   8 7 6 5 4 3 2 1 0 9